Scrambled Eggs and Whiskey

Hayden Carruth

Scrambled Eggs & Whiskey

POEMS, 1991–1995

COPPER CANYON PRESS

Publication of this book is supported by a grant from the National Endowment for the Arts and a grant from the Lannan Foundation. Additional support to Copper Canyon Press has been provided by the Andrew W. Mellon Foundation, the Lila Wallace–Reader's Digest Fund, and the Washington State Arts Commission. Copper Canyon Press is in residence with Centrum at Fort Worden State Park.

Library of Congress Cataloging-in-Publication Data
Carruth, Hayden, 1921–
Scrambled eggs and whiskey : poems, 1991–1995 / Hayden Carruth
p. cm.
ISBN 1-55659-109-8 (cloth) – ISBN 1-55659-110-1 (pbk.)
1. Title.
PS3505.A77594S57 1996
811'.54 – DC20   96-4487

9 8 7 6 5 4 3 2

COPPER CANYON PRESS

P.O. BOX 271, PORT TOWNSEND, WASHINGTON 98368

NOTE

THE WRITINGS in this book have all been done since the last ones in my *Collected Shorter Poems*, which was published in 1992. Otherwise I have no way of dating them, and the arrangement here is all but random. My wholehearted thanks to my friends who helped in making this selection: Adrienne Rich, Joe-Anne McLaughlin-Carruth, Len Roberts, Sam Hamill, and Stephen Dobyns.

H.C.

For Joe-Anne

Contents

Five-Thirty AM *3*

Flying into St. Louis *4*

Solemnization *5*

Wife Poem *6*

The Hyacinth Garden in Brooklyn *7*

Another *9*

The Soft Time of the Year *10*

Birthday Cake *11*

Quality of Wine *13*

Resorts *14*

California *15*

A Summer with Tu Fu *17*

Auburn Poem *30*

August 1945 *32*

Snow Storm *33*

Testament *35*

Endnote *37*

Folk Song: On the Road Again *38*

Forty-Five *40*

The Last Poem in the World *41*

Homage to Edwin Muir *42*

April Clean-Up *43*

I, I, I *44*

In Pharaoh's Tomb *45*

Bennington Poem *46*

Alteration *47*

Ecstasy *48*

February Morning *49*

The Woodcut on the Cover of Robert Frost's *Complete Poems* *51*

Particularity *52*

Rubaiyat *53*

Saturday at the Border *54*

Surrealism *55*

The Camps *57*

Swept *64*

The Best, the Most *65*
The Brook *66*
The Chain *67*
Isabel's Garden, May 14 *69*
Lilac Time *71*
The Curtain *72*
Window Blind *74*
Mort aux Belges! *75*
Pittsburgh *76*
Overlooking Pittsburgh *78*
Faxes to William *79*
Good Old Word Blues *86*
Graves *87*
Waterloo *88*
What to Do *89*
Notes on Poverty *90*
Song: Now That She is Here *91*
The Beat *92*
In the Long Hall *93*
The Woods *94*
This Morning *95*
Thorntrees *96*
In Georgetown *97*
Prepare *98*
Little Citizen, Little Survivor *100*
Scrambled Eggs and Whiskey *101*

Scrambled Eggs and Whiskey

Five-Thirty AM

Out the eastern window at
five-thirty this morning
are the pear tree, the sycamore,
and the high hill, the crest of it
with a new moon just risen
above it, a crescent tipped beyond
the dark trees, so clear and golden,
a jewel – yes, one might say a jewel –
and already behind it the first
dawnlight spreading faint and
soft and gray, like a mass of minute
dead angels' wings coming closer,
closer. The crescent is less bright.
Soon it will be invisible. Oh, there is
only an instant of vouchsafing!
What can one do but write this
little poem, finish the wine, take
the sleeping pills, and go to bed?

Flying into St. Louis

It is socked in. Can't see a thing. Nor have I ever
seen it before except once, driving east,
when I passed through at night
over the great river
and saw lights and the tremulous arch like a phantasm
through my off window. I was fighting
sleep, alone and desperate, as Americans so often are.
Yet my grandfather lived here.
I never saw him either
and my mother saw him only once after
she was two years old, which was when
he and my grandmother divorced
in 1898 in New York City –
a rarity then.
Years later my mother said, "He was a
seedy businessman in St. Louis." That's all.
A manufacturer of brandied cherries or souvenir ash trays?
I don't even know his name.
But seedy enough he was to beget my mother,
and thus one-quarter of my blood flowed from his veins,
one-quarter of my genes came from his testicles.
Is that where the madness came from then, the pain,
the desperation? For sixty-five years
I've blamed my mother and father,
I've climbed their trees and lopped off
their branches, I've held
their words in my mind like cudgels.
And it all may have been done
by the stranger from St. Louis
whose name I do not know.
I walked through the thronged corridor of the fog-bound terminal
alone and desperate
and boarded the plane to San Francisco.

Solemnization

On an old scroll we've read
half way, for there it faded
or rather the charactery
became foreign to us,
a rune, an ancient poetry
told us who we are: how
we are lovers not in the
exemplary of romance
but in the time of ruined
temples and foreboding
caves on the isle of Ararat,
and Prospero our governor.
I love you, Ariel. All
the others were vessels
of crazy lust, but you
in your bold youth are
a grace I haven't known,
an erotic decorum, your
body's magnanimity in
loving with an old man.
And I am Caliban for this
fable, which is not fabulous.

Wife Poem

And it's clear at last, she dropped
down from the moon, not like some
sylphy Cynthia at Delphi, after all she's
not seventeen, but with the sexual
grace and personal implacability
of a goddess of our time; so he says to
himself at night seeing the glow
of her sleep in her half (two-thirds really)
of their bed, the claire de lune of her shoulder
and forehead behind the deep clouds
of her hair. He drinks his wine
and swallows more pills. The birds
make their first aubade, little chirps and
chitterings, and outside the first light
mists their window. The day will be awful,
nervy and dull and sullen. His last
cigarette, his final gulp of chardonnay,
and he presses against her warm glow,
thinking of how he swam as a boy
of twelve in the warm pond beyond
the elms and hickories at the meadow's
edge. He turned like a sleepy carp among
the water lilies, under the dragonflies
and hot clouds of the old days of summer.

The Hyacinth Garden in Brooklyn

A year ago friends
    took me walking
on the esplanade
    in Brooklyn. I've
no idea where it
    was, I could never
find it on my own.
    And as we walked,
looking out over
    the water, a sweet
aroma came to us,
    heavy and rich,
of a hyacinth
    garden set
on the landward side
    among apartment
houses, a quite large
    garden with flowers
of every size and color,
    and the famous
perfume filled the air.
    It surrounded me,
dazed me, as I stood
    by the rail looking
down. There vaguely
    among the blooms
I saw Hyacinthus,
    the lovely African
boy beloved by Apollo,
    lying there, dying,
the dark body already
    rotting, melting
among flowers, bleeding
    in Brooklyn, in
Paradise, struck down

by the quoit thrown
by the grief-stricken god,
    an African boy
chosen for beauty, for love,
    for death, fragrance
beside the water
    on the esplanade
somewhere in Brooklyn,
    in Paradise.

Another

Let me say this finally
    in another little
song. Truth and beauty
    were never the
aims of proper poetry
    and the era
which proclaimed them
    was a brutal
era. Justice was what
    Homer sought
and Dante and Villon.
    We cannot
force it on these regressive
    Slavs or these
Indonesian murderers
    but in what is
ours, here, let
    justice be primary
when we sing,
    my dear.

The Soft Time of the Year

At last, at last the night
    lies down beneath the hill
and the busy city in the sky
    becomes visible. What
a bustling and confusion of
    activity up there! I
can see the rape of Helen
    and hear my own first cry
when I was born, for both
    of which I feel profoundly
sorry. Somewhere nearby
    meanwhile a paleolithic
relentless whippoorwill
    confides his commentary.

Birthday Cake

For breakfast I have eaten the last of your birthday cake that you
had left uneaten for five days
and would have left five more before throwing it away.
It is early March now. The winter of illness
is ending. Across the valley
patches of remaining snow make patterns among the hill farms,
among fields and knolls and woodlots,
like forms in a painting, as sure and significant as forms
in a painting. The cake was stale.
But I like stale cake, I even prefer it, which you don't
understand, as I don't understand how you can open
a new box of cereal when the old one is still unfinished.
So many differences. You a woman, I a man,
you still young at forty-two and I growing old at seventy.
Yet how much we love one another.
It seems a miracle. Not mystical, nothing occult,
just the ordinary improbability that occurs
over and over, the stupendousness
of life. Out on the highway on the pavement wet
with snow-melt, cars go whistling past.
And our poetry, yours short-lined and sounding
beautifully vulgar and bluesy
in your woman's bitterness, and mine almost
anything, unpredictable, though people say
too ready a harkening back
to the useless expressiveness and ardor of another
era. But how lovely it was, that time
in my restless memory.
This is the season of mud and trash, broken limbs and crushed briers
from the winter storms, wetness and rust,
the season of differences, articulable differences that signify
deeper and inarticulable and almost paleolithic
perplexities in our lives, and still
we love one another. We love this house
and this hillside by the highway in upstate New York.

I am too old to write love songs now. I no longer
assert that I love you, but that you love me,
confident in my amazement. The spring
will come soon. We will have more birthdays
with cakes and wine. This valley
will be full of flowers and birds.

Quality of Wine

This wine is really awful
I've been drinking for a year now, my
retirement, Rossi Chablis in a jug
from Oneida Liquors; plonk, the best
I can afford, awful. But at least
I can afford it, I don't need to go out and beg
on the street like the guys
on South Warren in Syracuse, eyes
burning in their sockets like acid.
And my sweetheart rubs my back when I'm
knotted in arthritis and swollen
muscles. The five stages of death
are fear, anger, resentment, renunciation,
and – ? Apparently the book doesn't say
what the fifth stage is. And neither
does the wine. Is it happiness? That's
what I think anyway, and I know I've been
through fear and anger and resentment and at least
part way through renunciation too, maybe
almost the whole way. A slow procedure,
like calling the Medicare office, on hold
for hours and then the recorded voice says, "Hang up
and dial again." Yet the days
hasten, they
go by fast enough. They fucking fly like the wind. Oh,
    Sweetheart, Mrs.
Manitou of the Stockbridge Valley,
my Red Head, my Absecon Lakshmi of the Marshlights,
my beautiful, beautiful Baby Doll,
let the dying be long.

Resorts

Remember when we visited Sylvan Beach
on Lake Oneida, the little sandpipers, color of dirt,
darting at the water's edge among sodden cigarette butts
and trash? In town were bad restaurants, truly bad,
with broken signboards. How all resort towns
by water are the same, we said. And the war
was exploding in the old Near East –
which still I am unable to write about,
the unbelievably enormous
concussions. I remember the same
in almost every year of my life, about which I have
written and written. All over the world old people
stand in line, anxious and bitter,
while the young gather in forlorn resentful gangs.
My dear, we are in love. It's a fact, certifiable.
It's a fact set there among the others, having
as much or as little significance as they,
whichever.

California

For Adrienne Rich

To come again into the place of revolutionary
thought after years in the wilderness
of complacency and hard-eyed greed
and brutality
is extraordinary. A.'s kitchen
in Santa Cruz
isn't greatly different from her kitchen in
West Barnet in the old days,
small interesting ornaments here and there,
many good things to eat –
and how ideas flew from stove to table,
from corner to corner. In Santa Cruz
after twenty-odd years it was the same. Tolstoi said
the purpose of poetry is to provoke
feeling in the reader, to "infect" the reader,
he said, – and so to induce a change,
a change of conscience
that may lead to a change in the world, that will
lead to a change in the world!
How can poetry be written by people who want no change?

To be reconciled after so long,
in sunshine, among Latino voices. A. showed me
where earthquake two years ago had changed Santa Cruz
and how the people were rebuilding, making it better. Had she
been frightened? Of course. Would she move away?
Never. Here earth itself gives us the paradigm.
And the great ocean hurling its might always thunderously against
the land at Half Moon Bay is our measure
of flux and courage
and eternity.

We drove among hills, redwood and eucalyptus,
dense growth, the richness and ramifying intricacy
of the world's loveliness, and asked
what would be left
for our grandchildren, already born, when they are
as old as we? No longer do we
need an insane president to end us
by pushing a button. People
need only go on living as they are, without change,
the complacent and hard-eyed
everywhere. At the airport
after dark
among hard lights
with the massive proportions of human energy
surrounding them, two old people
embraced in love of the injured and poor, of poetry,
of the world in its still remaining remote possibilities,
which were themselves.

A Summer with Tu Fu

for Sam Hamill

WHAT DOES IT MEAN?

What does it mean, master,
that across fifteen centuries
I make my profoundest and so fatally

inadequate obeisance to your
monarchic presence in the kingdom
of poetry? What does it mean

that two old guys speak to one another
from the sadnesses of exile,
confronting their final

futility after years of futile awkwardness
in the world of doing? We look,
you and I, at the heron in the sunset.

You have the advantage of a natural world
known in security, the mountain snow,
the village where the hens scratch

in familiar unchanging dust. And I
in the disappearing of my world
have the advantage of a beautiful

young woman, who is a poet too, to share
the moments of peace. We are not
the same, you and I, nor would I dare

presume, yet with you, as nothingness
descends and I fade away, I feel

a kinship I have not known before.

See how the heron folds her neck
in flight. See how mysteriously she perches
on the dead willow in her heraldic silence.

After all perhaps we are the same. Who can
the master be, who the apprentice? We embrace,
two smiling old men standing on the end of a pier.

THE CARDINAL

Strands of her red hair
sweat-stuck to her forehead
and a cardinal shrieks

in the dooryard. She is a poet
cooking supper on the hottest
afternoon of summer, toiling

in the book-lined kitchen.
What can an old man do
in return but make little

poems that will disappear
like the cardinal's shriek
when the night breeze rises?

THE LILIES

July is murderous. The heat makes
the maples still, their pleated leaves

hang down. The lilies bloom bright
orange like fire in the dooryard –

flames along the walk, the hedge,
orange tongues leaping in the corner.

News comes of the furious oppressors,
brutality abroad and at home.

Exiled by money, politics, and age,
he is exiled again by horror,

lying stiff and sweaty in his uncomfortable
hammock. At nightfall

the lilies die down and wither.
Nothing left, not even an ember.

SEA OF EXILE

Yes, as you say, the miseries of exile,
"as many as the pearls of the sea,"

wherever the sea is, wherever
the pearls. Billows,

combers, tides of greenery
crest over us – oaks

and black walnuts, maples,
sycamores, the fruit trees,

the vines, the immense grasses.
I am suffocating. Where

is the clean cool wind? Where are
the white triangular sails

on the horizon under racing clouds?
The dog yips in his sleep, the cats

hiss, contesting the territory
of the cooler tiles,

and Joe-Anne and I embrace wordlessly
in the kitchen, not knowing

if we are holding each other up
or pulling each other down.

It doesn't matter. The world seethes
inertly in a dry relentless tow.

[N.B. The quote is actually from Li Po.]

EMPIRE

The capitalist empire drove me here
to these gravelly hills where the elderberry
blooms raggedy white in the moonlight.

I despise you, court poets who drink
to forget your perfidy. I take a cup at bedtime
for sleep and the morning's remembering,

and I still cannot believe you wouldn't
give me a job when I needed one so badly.
May the system break and break, and take you

with it. Now in cold moonlight I crown my head
with elder leaves. But the moon here is not
the moon that shone on my old eastern home.

TO DAVID

We have no wide river, David, no
moon-track. When did we say goodbye?

We have no plum blossoms. Was it
ten years ago or more in the dark time

when I came in exile to these
measly hills under this friendless sky?

A long time and we've kept in touch. But not
by the warm stove with mugs of wine.

From your Green Mountains, David, send
one more poem to me before I die.

OLD SONG

An old song on a hot
midnight patio of summer.
"The House of the Rising Sun."

Look at the hazy stars
so soft in the coal-dark blue.
Cicadas. A woman singing.

DUCK FEATHER

The brook slow in August, murmuring.
White duck feather floating in a pool.

The meaning of a long summer afternoon.
No one can say it. Duck feather, dark water.

BOSNIA

This is the summer of war in Bosnia.
A few summers ago the war was somewhere else.

Four barn swallows swoop and swerve
like a string quartet across the lawn.

We forget sometimes that a shattered person
twists and cries and dies like a dog or a woodchuck.

Flesh ripped apart, ragged, bloody. Violent sex
is what war is and what the warriors are.

In Frankfort near Utica where
Sara Anne Wood, a child of twelve,

has disappeared, her bicycle thrown in the weeds,
her books and papers scattered. She has been gone

for three weeks, stolen away to what
miseries of mind and body?

We watch the swallows. We wait for rain.
Unspoken thoughts lie heavy on the afternoon.

HOT GARDEN ON COMSTOCK

In a hot garden the steel-gray cat crouches,
springs quick as a frog-tongue, snatches

the butterfly, then hunkers down
to eat it. Bright wings disappearing.

Thunder. Black clouds roiling overhead
in the heat like the crowns of some

gigantic forest. The young woman says she
doesn't care what happens to her body

as long as her mind is intact. A stench
of neighboring compost drifts on the bouquet

of spicy meat. Laughter and politics. Truly we are
the wise animals. Just not wise enough.

ANOTHER JOURNEY

Another journey. The southern provinces,
Pennsylvania. I think also of you

in your wandering exile. What are
the differences? Perhaps only

the speed of change. A swallow here
zooms across the pond, becoming

a winter jay on the farther shore.
Snow whirls in the pass, torrential

rain drenches the cabbage fields,
the palace grounds are enshrouded

with mist. Old age and final illness
come with the swiftness of the Yangtze

flooding in springtime, or like
the quick unreeling cinematograph.

CONTENTED GOD

At night the red ball
drifts back and forth
in the swimming pool

silently in the merest
stirring of how and why
and shall and could

as if it were
the embodied spirit
of some contented god.

DIFFERENCES

A peach and a nectarine taste
the same, but they're not

– not quite – and some folk swear
by the difference.

You and I
know where to place our minds.

THE STORM

Distant thunder at night rumbles
down the valley. Far lightning

flickers on the ceiling. The first
heavy raindrops make pock-sounds

on the tin roof. He reaches between
her legs and holds the hot moist

softness there and at once reposes
in the comforting world of the coming storm.

EVENING

The evening rain is over. The flowers
begin to raise their heads. What book

shall I read tomorrow? Over what
deathless poem will I fall asleep? Won't

these crickets ever shut up! Straining broken
cork from my wine with broken teeth.

FRANCONIA

Old friend, you used to read your poems
to a few acquaintances, to the Abbot
in your drifting boat, to your neighbor Mr. Li.

In Franconia in an old barn I read poems
with my beautiful young auburn-haired wife
to a couple of hundred students and townspeople.

How they loved us, we two. My wife's poems
are like old eastern sorrow-songs
from the lowland by the edge of the oily

sea. Sparrows chirped in the rafters, moths
wandered in and out among shafts of moonlight.
Home is wherever these odd moments

snag our raft on the slow river of exile.
I was as happy, as gratified, as ever I've been,
old friend, in all these seventy-two years.

I think of you in Chiang-tang, there beyond
the Wei, reading in the night to Li Po.
Nothing can be better than two poets together.

PEACE ON THE WATER

Tu Fu, you were in my thoughts last night
while I was on the wide water of Toronto Bay.

Herons flew among the islands and settled
with wide wings in the silvery treetops.

In the twilight the lighted city shone
like a jewel on the distant shore.

I imagined you in your skiff on the broad
River of the Yellow Moon, how still

the water lay, how you paused and listened
to the frogs conversing among the reeds.

Michael Callaghan's boat chugged slowly
into gathering darkness and faint lights glistened

in my wife's auburn hair where she sat alone
on the foredeck like the Queen of the Mists.

ISABEL'S GARDEN

You would like Isabel's garden, old friend, this vista
of green horizontals and verticals – the yew, dogwood,
larch, locust, juniper – the lawns and walks, even

a Chinese gate, and then these flowers, not so many
blooming now in this hot depth of summer,
a few lilies – white, orange, red – the English daisies,

the impatiens and aromatic phlox. We could
sit here in quiet, in peace. The city would be only
like a murmuring waterfall far beyond us.

We could drink our cool wine and talk of poems,
of our children and our distant grandchildren.
You could read me what you wrote this morning.

Isabel Bize from Chile has made this garden.
You would like her too. How gratefully similar minds
come together from all times and places.

DEAD PULP

After a lifetime of self-loathing, finally
this. For days he wears only his ragged

undershorts, which ought to be against the law.
What was strong once and reasonably

good-looking has gone to sag and shrivel
and adiposity in the sweltering heat.

The big trucks grind sluggishly up the hill
carrying dead pulp to the paper mill.

THE DOVE

In an instant the dove was shot from its perch
in a burst of feathers. Loneliness struck.

Alienation. Quelle douleur, cher maître,
que je vous vois, mais vous ne pouvez me voir.

THE HEAVINESS

Language is defeated
in the heavy, heavy day.

Limp lines on the page
like grass mown in the meadow.

Only the sparrows
chatter among the vines.

THE WAY

Was it the way of your world too,
old master, that everyone had to be
a villain in someone else's life?

It is the way of ours apparently. Such
is the pressure of evil on our spirits now.
This poor woman whom I never harmed

hates me passionately. Why? I know
your emperor was not averse to beheadings.
Terror unwinds forever from the bobbin

of history, and in the moonlight I can see
your sad, placid, misty river. I recall your words
of poverty and exile. Who knows what is true?

CONVERSING

Old men converse across the abyss of time
on a hot evening in elusive lights –

you there by the Peach Blossom River,
I here overlooking the Stockbridge Valley.

Darkness everywhere. The river lapping
at the shore, traffic muted in the valley.

How much I value this friendship!
I raise my glass of ice-cold chardonnay.

END OF SUMMER

September 2nd. How swift, how swift! The bank
has been painted with goldenrod by a mysterious

celebrated painter. Ah, but we reject that nonsense,
old friend, do we not? This summer with you

has been such a warm, reasonable, companionable
time, let us be grateful. Let us rejoice

in the pristine yellow of newly blossoming flowers,
and there – the beginning purple of the aster bush.

Soon the bank will be heaped with snow. The wind
from the west will scour this valley till it shines

in frozen flawlessness. I wonder, shall we share a glass
on this pine plank when the grass is green next summer?

Auburn Poem

A book I was reading this morning
by Milan Kundera contains this: "In the algebra
of love a child is the symbol of the magical

sum of two beings." And now that child
is thirty-nine years old; she is suffering
from a cancer which we are told is incurable

and will become fatal. You have been married
for thirty years to another man, and I
have been married to three other women

and have lived with six whom I did not
marry – a disgrace but there it is, done
and irrevocable. We are old. You are

sixty-nine and I am seventy. It would be
sentimental folly to say I can see in you,
or you in me, the lineaments of our

loving youth. Yet it is true. Your voice
especially takes me back. We are here
because our daughter, whom we conceived

one fine April night in Chicago long ago,
is crucially vulnerable. We meet in agony,
in wordless despair. We meet after years

of separation and mildly affectionate
unconcern. But it's true, true, this child
who is a mature, afflicted woman

with children of her own, is still a symbol
of that magical sum we were, and in this
wretchedness, without word or touch or hidden

glance, I hold myself out to you, and I know
I am accepted without word or touch or hidden
glance. This, so late, the crisis of our lives.

August 1945

Sweating and greasy in the dovecote where one of them lived
    four young men drank "buzzy" from canteen cups, the drink
made from warm beer mixed half-and-half with colorless Italian
    distilled alcohol. A strange fierce taste like bees in the mouth.
Their faces gleamed in the light of a single candle. They were
    getting drunk, deliberately, for this was the only answer. They
sang songs of joy, they sang "Lili Marlene," they were silent,
    they broke into sobbing. They spoke of home, thousands
of miles away, of the years of filth and fear and loneliness,
    of war and war's ending, of the new bomb that had killed
hundreds of thousands at one blow in Japan. There near
    Manfredonia on the Adriatic coast, across from Ithaka where
Odysseus the Wise had once come home from war, in the huge
    disordered repple-depple where throngs of men had waited,
milling and shuffling, shuffling and milling, for shipment
    to the war in Asia, these four were delirious, dumbfounded.
Gratefully they slipped away, falling into the discontinuity
    and incoherence of drunkenness. In a tiny room perched high
on a wall over a courtyard, over a dark field where fires burned
    and cries resounded, the night so hot, the air so evil-smelling,
candlelight flickered on the slack faces of four young men,
    ravaged and stuporous, who knew that time had stopped
        and started again.

Snow Storm

Everywhere men speak in whispers.
Tumult, many new ghosts. Storm
hurls itself across the valley
and careens from the ridges, swirls
of snow lapsing, leaping, colliding.
Outside on the highway a car
has rolled over the guard-rail,
two pickups have stopped, men
stand hunched with their hands
in their pockets. We are looking
from our kitchen windows, we
have called the county sheriff
and the wrecker, we have asked
the men to come in for coffee.
But they have said no, somewhat
sullenly. Earlier we had been speaking
of war in the Persian Gulf, of
all the wars and how armies are
everywhere now, hardly one
peaceful corner remaining
in the world. In strange cities
and in wastelands, on mountains
and on islands, young men and women
in clumsy uniforms and in unease
stand hunched with their hands
in their pockets, or drink
as much beer as they can, or screw
themselves silly – but mostly
they stand hunched with their hands
in their pockets, scornful of the native
people. Now through the snow
the men on the highway are vague
distant figures in a veiled world,
the car's lights are dim and unclear.

In our eaves and around our dormers
the wind cries and moans with increased
force, and the night comes on.

Testament

So often has it been displayed to us, the hourglass
with its grains of sand drifting down,
not as an object in our world
but as a sign, a symbol, our lives
drifting down grain by grain,
sifting away – I'm sure everyone must
see this emblem somewhere in the mind.
Yet not only our lives drift down. The stuff
of ego with which we began, the mass
in the upper chamber, filters away
as love accumulates below. Now
I am almost entirely love. I have been
to the banker, the broker, those strange
people, to talk about unit trusts,
annuities, CDS, IRAS, trying
to leave you whatever I can after
I die. I've made my will, written
you a long letter of instructions.
I think about this continually.
What will you do? How
will you live? You can't go back
to cocktail waitressing in the casino.
And your poetry? It will bring you
at best a pittance in our civilization,
a widow's mite, as mine has
for forty-five years. Which is why
I leave you so little. Brokers?
Unit trusts? I'm no financier doing
the world's great business. And the sands
in the upper glass grow few. Can I leave
you the vale of ten thousand trilliums
where we buried our good cat Pokey
across the lane to the quarry?
Maybe the tulips I planted under
the lilac tree? Or our red-bellied

woodpeckers who have given us so
much pleasure, and the rabbits
and the deer? And kisses? And
love-makings? All our embracings?
I know millions of these will be still
unspent when the last grain of sand
falls with its whisper, its inconsequence,
on the mountain of my love below.

Endnote

The great poems of
our elders in many
tongues we struggled

to comprehend who
are now content with
mystery simple

and profound you
in the night your
breath your body

orbit of time and
the moment you
Phosphorus and

Hesper a dark circle
of fertility so
bloodthirsty for us

you in the world
the night breathing
asleep and alive.

Folk Song: On the Road Again

Pennsylvania in early spring.
Daffodils yellow by the fences.
   Different from home
       where the earth
still struggles to throw off
       winter's bedraggled
coverlet.
    I went walking up Len's hill
with Len's black dog named Magic
    after Magic Johnson looking
along the hedgerows for wildflowers,
anything springlike I thought –
    bloodroot, skunk cabbage, or
       arbutus hiding,
but found only one little heal-all
       in the fraught grass.
    I was thinking of my wife
at home in the dying winter, I was
    thinking of Odysseus wandering,
of Dr. Williams when he came to Chicago
after his first stroke, after he had
       "recovered," how
he had gone sleepless on the Pullman,
how he trembled, how he was afraid.
    And where was Floss? Why had he
       left her at home?
Why was Penny O. in Ithaka all those years
    and not on the beaches of Ilion?
Why is Joe-Anne not here when I
    go walking on Len's hill alone
with Magic and my heart attack
       trembling in my chest?
Did Dr. Williams leave Floss at home
in Rutherford to spare her the second
    stroke – the crisis on the road?

Why does the thought of Ovid
    in exile on the Thracian shore
        waiting for death
linger in my mind these years of my
        own approaching
        final solitude?
Why when certitude was promised
    does my mind dwindle like this
        to questioning?
Why in Pennsylvania in early spring
        is it so cold?

Forty-Five

When I was forty-five I lay for hours
beside a pool, the green hazy
springtime water, and watched
the salamanders coupling, how they drifted lazily,
their little hands floating before them,
aimlessly in and out of the shadows, fifteen
or twenty of them, and suddenly two
would dart together and clasp
one another belly to belly
the way we do, tender and vigorous, and then
would let go and drift away
at peace, lazily,
in the green pool that was their world
and for a while was mine.

The Last Poem in the World

Would I write it if I could?
Bet your glitzy ass I would.

Homage to Edwin Muir

Every day I drive Pratt's Road
    Along the valley floor where fall
These green waves of the long-cooled earth,
    "And small is great and great is small
        And the blind seed all."

From Bear Path Road across the flats
    Of tacky prefabricated houses,
And past the old farms farther on,
    Past the bank where the groundhog rouses,
        The pool where a gray goose grieves and browses.

Thence to Pratt's Hollow soon I come,
    One empty church and a tavern dark
Which, a few evenings every week
    To entice the farmers after work,
        Hangs out a sign just saying "Pork."

In similar anecdotes you and I
    Would give this place a smitch of fame,
Would give ourselves some trifling notion
    Of why we're here and why we came
        And why Pratt's Hollow has a name.

It doesn't. Not a name that counts.
    The blind seed is anonymous.
It gives us time but never place,
    What is, what might be, not what was.
        And it is all of us.

April Clean-up

He isn't quite a eunuch but that's
what he calls himself, this old
two-beat codger on this spring
afternoon picking up the winter's
crop of twigs and bark from the lawn
to make it "look nicer" and to supply
the house with kindling next winter
for himself or his heirs, meanwhile coughing
and gasping, cursing the pain in his back,
thinking always of the days when
each year after the run-off he was in
the woods with the early trout lilies
and violets and with his ax, saw,
and canthook, doing a man's work
that has no connection with sex at all.

I, I, I

First, the self. Then, the observing self.
The self that acts and the self that watches. This
The starting point, the place where the mind begins,
Whether the mind of an individual or
The mind of a species. When I was a boy
I struggled to understand. For if I know
The self that watches, another watching self
Must see the watcher, then another seeing that,
Another and another, and where does it end?
And my mother sent me to the barber shop,
My first time, to get my hair "cut for a part"
(Instead of the dutch boy she'd always given me),
As I was instructed to tell the barber. She
Dispatched me on my own because the shop,
Which had a pool table in the back, in that
Small town was the men's club, and no woman
Would venture there. Was it my first excursion
On my own into the world? Perhaps. I sat
In the big chair. The wall behind me held
A huge mirror, and so did the one in front,
So that I saw my own small strange blond head
With its oriental eyes and turned up nose repeated
In ever diminishing images, one behind
Another behind another, and I tried
To peer farther and farther into the succession
To see the farthest one, diminutive in
The shadows. I could not. I sat rigid
And said no word. The fat barber snipped
My hair and blew his brusque breath on my nape
And finally whisked away his sheet, and I
Climbed down. I ran from that cave of mirrors
A mile and a half to home, to my own room
Up under the eaves, which was another cave.
It had no mirrors. I no longer needed mirrors.

In Pharaoh's Tomb

In Pharaoh's tomb the darkness reigns.
    The air was stale and musty.
A thief broke in and stole his eyes
    and was not even stealthy.

Pharaoh saw less than he had seen
    before, which seems unlikely.
"Ah what have I ever done to thee
    that thou so indiscreetly

should'st rob my face?" great Pharaoh cried.
    But the robber was undaunted.
"Shut up, old man. Go back to sleep.
    Vision's not what you wanted."

Bennington Poem

Through the forest, the big busy
greenness on either side, dark and dark...
And the road narrowed to a track
with grass growing on it, a lane
in the wilderness. We thought
maybe it will end entirely, fade
out, and we'll have to find a way
to turn and go back, which would be
difficult and even dangerous, but
neither of us said this. Scared but not
afraid, our p'tit malaise en Amérique;
and we drove on for miles and miles,
with soft touchings close together,
through the green and dark in silence.
White pine, maple, ash, and beech;
hazel, hobblebush, and moosewood;
mallow and knapweed in the grass.
Three sensible coyotes trotted by us
like dogs on a street in Syracuse.
I thought how love, that had nearly
all my life been an absence, was now
a presence. At last, hours later, a sign,
Collinsville, a settlement perched on
the edge of the notch of the mountain –
Stratton Mountain singing in the low
tones of Windigo and St. Malachy –
five or six poor houses, and we knew we
weren't lost, the track with no fork
which had seemed sometimes to be
waning away had brought us through
safely. Our little anxiety had been un-
necessary. Yet then we looked at one
another – in our little abatement –
and knew without saying that we still
wished we hadn't come to Collinsville.

Alteration

You thought growing older
    would be more of the same,
going a little slower,
    walking a little lame.

But you knew, or you were a fool,
    that alteration is what we keep;
tonight will not be the equal
    of last night, even in sleep.

Ecstasy

For years it was in sex and I thought
this was the most of it
               so brief
                         a moment
or two of transport out of oneself
                        or
in music which lasted longer and filled me
with the exquisite wrenching agony
of the blues
              and now it is equally
transitory and obscure as I sit in my broken
chair that the cats have shredded
by the stove on a winter night with wind and snow
howling outside and I imagine
the whole world at peace
                   at peace
and everyone comfortable and warm
the great pain assuaged
                       a moment
of the most shining and singular sensual gratification.

February Morning

The old man takes a nap
too soon in the morning.
His coffee cup grows cold.

Outside the snow falls fast.
He'll not go out today.
Others must clear the way

to the car and the shed.
Open upon his lap
lie the poems of Mr. Frost.

Somehow his eyes get lost
in the words and the snow,
somehow they go

backward against the words,
upward among the flakes
to the great silence of air,

the blank abundance there.
Should he take warning?
Mr. Frost went off, they say,

in bitterness and despair.
The old man stirs and wakes,
hearing the hungry birds,

nuthatch, sparrow, and jay,
clamor outside, unfed,
and words stir from his past

like this agitated sorrow
of jay, nuthatch, and sparrow,
classical wrath which takes

no shape now in a song.
He climbs the stairs to bed.
The snow falls all day long.

The Woodcut on the Cover of
Robert Frost's COMPLETE POEMS

For Wendell Berry

A man plowing starts at the side of the field
Nearer home and works outward and away.
Why? Because plowing is always an adventure.
Then walking home with the horses at end of day.

Particularity

How it is blurring, oozing
    slowly away from
me. This is an
    awful moment

every time. The grove
    of sumac I've known
so long becoming
    a lump of

undifferentiated land-
    scape, like the fallen
barn and the hill
    itself. Then

everything is one,
    is nothing. Only
here is left, here –
    this invisible

hereness where I am,
    where I am
existing, here, the center
    of mystery.

Rubaiyat

Omar, Tu Fu, and I were on the pier
At Tenth Street drinking vodka and warm beer
And writing verses, turn and turn about,
And floating them downriver with a cheer.

Saturday at the Border

Here I am writing my first villanelle
At seventy-one, and feeling old and tired –
"Hey, pops, why dontcha just give us the old death-knell?" –

And writing it what's more on the rim of hell
In blazing Arizona when all I desired
Was north and solitude and not a villanelle,

Working from memory and not remembering well
How many stanzas and in what order, wired
On Mexican coffee, seeing the death-knell

Of sun's salvos upon these hills that yell
Bloody murder silently to the much admired
Dead-blue sky. One wonders if a villanelle

Can do the job. Yes, old men now must tell
Our young world how these bigots and these retired
Bankers of Arizona are ringing the death-knell

For all of us, how ideologies compel
Children to violence. Artifice acquired
For its own sake is war. Frail Villanelle,

Have you this power? And must I go and sell
Myself? "Wow," they say, and "cool" – this hired
Old poetry guy with his spaced out death-knell.

Ah, far from home and God knows not much fired
By thoughts of when he thought he was inspired,
He writes by writing what he must. Death-knell
Is what he's found in his first villanelle.

Surrealism

for Charlie Simic

Oof! Another summer morning with the air
so thick it makes your teeth wrinkle and your toes

stop talking to one another. So a mourning
dove – one of them clumsy perchers – lights

teeteringly on the wire that runs from the house
to the corner maple where it connects

with another wire crossing the drive
to the garage. Poor old gray garage, leaning

unfeasibly in two directions from the heavy
run-off each spring on this northern hill.

All perfectly normal. Then the first wire broke,
and the second, and the garage collapsed

sideways like a fat senator loaded with scotch
on the state house lawn. The dove flew off

to the sycamore and went uuu-uuu'u-uuu
like the Pope on his balcony broadcasting Peace,

and I cried, "Si j'avais une bombe…!"* I
grabbed my answering machine and ran out,

and I let that dove have it full bore, *leave your*
message after the beep, leave your message

* "*Si j'avais une bombe…!*" A graffito I saw on the side of a bank in Privas in 1977.

after the beep, and by God one less perjuring
capitalist of death was left in this world.

The Camps

For Marilyn Hacker

"Yes, art is palliative; but the substance of art is real.
Can you make something from nothing?"
– *Ivan Tolkachenko*

When the young brown-haired
woman was shot
a drop of blood swayed
briefly
on the end of her nose
and her baby brother for an instant
thought of a lantern.

      *   *   *

As the kittens were born
the father of the little girl
bashed the head
of each one against a rock.
She watched. This was
in another country. It was
in several other countries.

      *   *   *

The town is divided between those
who sit in a dark corner of what remains
of their houses
unwilling to see anyone
and those who go out into what remains
of the street
unwilling not to see everyone.

      *   *   *

A sparrow flew into the high loft
above the people lying on the floor
and fluttered here and there crying
and cheeping as if trying to drink
the light at the crevices but at last
perched on a broken concrete strut
and closed its eyes.

* * *

The small pile of starved children
resembles the pile of brush
at the edge of a woods
in Alaska. Each will recede
into the earth at about
the same rate as the other.

* * *

Some always say the cats
or the crows or the ants
will be last,
but some insist
that the tough young women
and men will somehow endure,
will somehow prevail.

* * *

After they arrived
they spoke inventively in their language for a long time,
weeks and weeks,
contriving new snappy names for hunger,
for God and Satan,
for the machine,
until the subject itself faltered, and they were silent.

* * *

For a second after the
sweep of bullets
he looked at himself cut in half.

* * *

Who is it that stalks the camp?
Not the commandant, he has more sense.
Not the garbage-picker, there is no garbage.
Not that dying baobab tree over there.
Not the dew, there is no dew.
Not even the memory of the dew.
Yet we who are women bury our heads
in our hair and are still.
We who are children sprawl on the earth.
We who are men fold our hands and fall back
with our eyes wide.
Nobody knows who it is that stalks the camp.

* * *

I am dying because I am black, one says.
Or because I am poor.
Or because I speak bad Spanish or Arabic.
Or because they found me in the Third Street Bar.
Or because my husband ran away.
You see, we are of the world in spite of everything
and we cling to the world's reasons.

* * *

A little way apart from the long trudging
line of prisoners, a woman lay down
in the snow and gave birth. She was a sad
good-looking blonde. But I am not a woman,

she says. I cannot be, I refuse. Who is this dead
woman lying in the snow? No, I am a coyote.
And at once all the prisoners cried out softly
the coyote's song, which fills the gray air
from horizon to horizon and settles
upon the world. The newborn
coyote pup scampers away over the snow,
across the plain, into the forest.

* * *

Most of the starving children die peacefully
in their weakness, lying passive and still.
They themselves are as unaware of their
passing away as everyone else. But a few
haggard boys and girls at the last moment
twitch and open their eyes, and a sound
comes from their throats. Their eyes
express if only faintly, knowledge
of their private dearness about to be
extinguished. They are struck by their superb
identities. Yes, these are the ones who....

* * *

The world was never unbeautiful. All its parts,
marsh and savannah, forest and lake, scars
of lava and lightning and erosion, sparkled
in the sun. Now it has this camp and that one
and the thousands of others, camps almost
everywhere. Even the word *camp* once meant a field.

* * *

Sometimes children
become playthings.
A bit of their

intestines is pulled
out and handed
to them to see what
they will do with it.

    * * *

When an artillery shell falls
in a particular neighborhood, what follows
is an immediate exodus of body parts and other furniture,
and then the slower exodus. Usually
old people and children, but others too,
maimed and ill, mothers and cousins,
friends and strangers – an unlikely company – walking
in file, weak and unsteady, harried sometimes
by armed guards or sometimes not,
walking, walking, shuffling
through alleys, plazas, across bridges, out
along dusty roads, across the fields,
into the hills and forests.

    * * *

Following at a distance or waiting
in the shadows are wild dogs. Scream
if you can. Beg to be shot.

    * * *

And some are left behind, always in every village,
undiscovered, like this woman of forty
whose origin is doubtful. Is she black, white,
brown, yellow, pink? She is speckled.
Once she was plump and now her skin
sags around her like folds of dirty woolen
though she is nearly naked, and her wrinkled
dugs fall sideways where she is lying, her leg is

61

gangrenous, already part of the shinbone is showing
unexpectedly white. She is waiting for the sunrise
to bring her a little warmth while she
watches herself become a skeleton.

* * *

He who is writing these words, an old man
on an undistinguished hillside
in North America
who has been writing for sixty years because this
is his way of being in the world, writing
on scraps of paper with stubby pencils
or on cheap tablets from the drug store, on a battered typewriter
set on an orange crate in a roach-ridden flat
in Chicago or in a small country house
on a computer, writing
all his life long
in the desert, on the mountain, in the forest,
on a beautiful boulder standing in the middle of a mountain brook,
writing,
writing year after year the way robins
build their nests…
What if these were his last words?
What if these sentences should be the vision at the end
of a lifetime he could never alter?

* * *

Sing then of love
in the camps. Somebody
gives somebody else
a swallow of water.
People hold hands,
a woman cuddles her
baby as long as
she can. Men in the face

of the sweeping automatic
rifles against the wall
embrace just before
the blast. And does it
help? Ah how ardent
the hope has been! But
no one knows, the evidence
has vanished.

    * * *

In the simple tableau two brown women
lie with their hands
between each other's legs, worn-out
fingers resting in vulvas, a child
of eight or nine, turned aside, its sex
unknown, fondles itself but the arm fails
and drops down, a wife lies
with her husband's limp penis
against her cheek. Over the camp like descending
twilight the remnants of love
rest on the unmoving forms.

Swept

When we say I
miss you what
we mean is I'm
filled with

dread. At night
alone going
to bed is
like lying down

in a wave. Total
absence of light.
Swept away to
gone.

The Best, the Most

Yet one young woman lives with me
and is my love. She's my bride and she's
beautiful and has had many lovers
in New Mexico and the East. What

can this verify except that she, of all
who said they loved me, loves me
most and best? She loves me for
myself, or for what little is left,

and she is passionate. True, I've noticed
in who knows how many poems this life
is hell, the inferno of every day, every
miserable day, but not the reborn's

pitchfork in the kidneys. It has its joy
in pain, in sorrow its contentment,
which is old age given to love, failing
and failing, falling, ruined, rich.

The Brook

Murmuring of the brook in late
summer darkness, after moonset,
as I lay sleepless on the porch cot.
A music extraordinarily variable.
Each passage of water against its stone
sounding a different pitch and rhythm.
It was an uncivilized music in the
foothills of the mountains, continuing
long beyond the endurance of a human
singer, almost beyond the endurance
of a human listener, syllables
of unknown meaning, notes on an
unknown scale. A few fat yellow
stars above the northern horizon.
Without art, the song was perfectly
artistic. The unmeaning music
and the unknowing listener were one
in the loneliness of those distant
late summer nights in Vermont.
Truly the music meant nothing,
no intimation, which was why
I liked it so much, my brook
murmuring all night in the darkness,
and I meant nothing, and I liked that too.

The Chain

This was the time of year, time of the last relentless snows
and mud and ice, when I died and was convulsed
back to life by the shocks of technologists
as if by the fires of hell. And you came to me,
a friend from the past. You brought
a thin gold chain
which you linked around my wrist, saying, "This
will bind you to life." Later when we were lovers
the chain augmented for us and became the sign
of our binding together, and when we married,
more than the rings our chain
was our incorporating. Then it broke. It snagged
and the links let loose. You gave me another
made of stronger links, and you said
the same words in the giving. Now after two more years
this chain has broken too, just as words
break, as this poem
will break. How we long for peace. How we cherish
the dove on the peaceful flag
even while the real doves at our bird-feeder
fight viciously among themselves
and against the smaller sparrows, finches, and chickadees
for the seed I place there in abundance.
The dove on the flag is more real for us,
as this poem in breaking
words is real though its motive force can never
be brought forth to our eyes. I hope you will
give me another chain. I know I am bound
to life and to you
but I am a poet and you are too and so are all people
except the monsters of this world
out there planting
mines in the mud and snow. We must continually
guard and cherish the endangered frail dove,

our breaking words,
our chain,
every instrument and emblem of this world's love.

Isabel's Garden, May 14

For Isabel Bize

The fruit trees are in full bloom.
Apple, crabapple, the dogwood tree
at work on its small inedible berry.
It's a flowering above eye-level, a warm
iridescent mist, beneath which the tulips
have begun to fall, their heads tousled
and frowzy; and elsewhere are
forget-me-nots, bluets, the first verbenas,
spreading patches of grape hyacinths,
rock pinks, a few white trilliums,
and other flowers, exotic beauties
from the seed catalogues – Isabel knows
their names but I can never remember.
Isabel is slender and beautiful and today
she is gardening in a pale blue blouse
and a long dark blue flowered skirt
with earrings and a necklace and lipstick.
She says she felt low this morning, so
she dressed up to work in her garden,
which is characteristic and perfectly sincere.
She looks as elegant as her flowers,
a companion to them. And what am
I, an old man on the porch peering
out at the world with a portable
computer on his lap, his scant hairs
tousled too, hands spotted and stiff,
brain hurting from too much drink
last night? And what is this poem – is it
necessity or an exercise? I am too old
to think about this any more. The poem
has grown on this screen like a flower,
letter by letter, cell by cell, color by
color, assuming its own brief

identity in the efflorescence. I am
the inelegant gardener soiling my
hands in the humus of the alphabet.

Lilac Time

The winter was fierce, my dear,
    Snowy and blowy and cold,
A heart-breaker and record-breaker,
    And I am feeble and old.

But now it is lilac time.
    Come out in the sweet warm air,
Come and I'll gather flowers
    To put in your beautiful hair.

Let's make a bouquet of lilac
    For our old bedside table.
Then the fragrance in the night
    Will make me form-i-dable.

The Curtain

Just over the horizon a great machine of death is roaring and rearing.

We can hear it always. Earthquake, starvation, the ever-renewing sump
of corpse-flesh.

But in this valley the snow falls silently all day, and out our window

We see the curtain of it shifting and folding, hiding us away in our
little house,

We see earth smoothened and beautified, made like a fantasy, the
snow-clad trees

So graceful. In our new bed, which is big enough to seem like the
north pasture almost

With our two cats, Cooker and Smudgins, lying undisturbed in the
southeastern and southwestern corners,

We lie loving and warm, looking out from time to time. "Snowbound,"
we say. We speak of the poet

Who lived with his young housekeeper long ago in the mountains of
the western province, the kingdom

Of cruelty, where heads fell like wilted flowers and snow fell for many
months

Across the pass and drifted deep in the vale. In our kitchen the maple-
fire murmurs

In our stove. We eat cheese and new-made bread and jumbo Spanish
olives

Which have been steeped in our special brine of jalapeños and garlic
and dill and thyme.

We have a nip or two from the small inexpensive cognac that makes us
smile and sigh.

For a while we close the immense index of images that is our lives – for
instance,

The child on the Mescalero reservation in New Mexico sitting naked
in 1966 outside his family's hut,

Covered with sores, unable to speak. But of course we see the child ev-
ery day,

We hold out our hands, we touch him shyly, we make offerings to his
implacability.

No, the index cannot close. And how shall we survive? We don't and
cannot and will never

Know. Beyond the horizon a great unceasing noise is undeniable. The
machine,

Like an immense clanking vibrating shuddering unnameable contrap-
tion as big as a house, as big as the whole town,

May break through and lurch into our valley at any moment, at any
moment.

Cheers, baby. Here's to us. See how the curtain of snow wavers and
then falls back.

Window Blind

You keep the blind of our north window drawn.
Night after night we snuggle here and hold
each other in our reclusive unison
under our heavy blankets from Hudson's Bay
as if we were two clarinets beneath
the world's cellos and basses. We are devoid
of essence, two existences, thus neither
old nor young, male nor female, flesh nor stone,
which in existing and by existing are
only, onely, perfect – or nearly so.
Our song is a happy purring song. And yet
the blind is always drawn and at the back
of my mind I wonder why – why you at morning
dismiss the one clean pure light in the world
that comes to us from the north beyond the north,
from clarity there, unseen, unfaltering, and true.

Mort aux Belges!

Consider the administration of
    justice in what was called the Belgian
Congo. If one man was convicted
    of thievery or irreligion

the soldiers went into his village
    and amputated the right hands
of all the inhabitants, men, women,
    and children, so that on the weekend

if you visited you'd find a circle
    of empty huts and in the center
on the beaten earth right hands heaped
    in a little pile for you to encounter

on your journey and think of those who
    lost them, helpless in the forest, children
probably bled to death – a village
    in every possible way abandoned.

Pittsburgh

And my beautiful daughter
had her liver cut open in Pittsburgh.
My god, my god! I rubbed
her back over the swollen and wounded
essentiality, I massaged
her legs, and we talked of death.
At the luckiest patients with liver cancer have
a 20% chance. We might have talked
of my death, not long to come. But no,
the falling into death of a beautiful
young woman is so much more important.
A wonderful hospital. If I must die
away from my cat Smudge and my Vermont Castings stove
let it be at Allegheny General.
I read to her, a novella by Allan Gurganus,
a Russian serious flimsiness by Voinovich,
and we talked. We laughed. We actually
laughed. I bought her a lipstick
which she wore though she disliked the color.
Helicopters took off and landed on the hospital pad,
bringing hearts and kidneys and maybe livers
from other places to be transplanted
into people in the shining household of technology
by shining technologists, wise and kindly.
The chances are so slight. Oh, my daughter,
my love for you has burgeoned –
an excess of singularity ever increasing –
you are my soul – for forty years. You
still beautiful and young. In my hotel
I could not sleep. In my woods, on my
little farm, in the blizzard on the mountain,
I could not sleep either, but scribbled
fast verses, very fast and
wet with my heartsblood and brainjuice
all my life, as now

in Pittsburgh. I don't know which of
us will live the longer, it's all a flick
of the wrist of the god mankind invented
and then had to deinvent, such a failure, like all
our failures, and the worst and best
is sentimentality after all. Let us go out together.
Here in brutal Pittsburgh. Let us
be together in the same room,
the old poet and the young painter,
holding hands, a calm touch, a whisper,
as the thumping helicopters go out and come in,
we in the crisis of forever inadequately medicated
pain, in the love of daughter and father.

Overlooking Pittsburgh

You wanted to paint Pittsburgh
from the window at the end
of the high hospital corridor, old wooden
houses jumbled on the hill,
shapes like nature brought to
ideal abstraction by the hill's excess,
colors like imagination raised
to nature's quiet perfect grandeur –
yellow, green, brown, slate,
subtle ocher. Sweet good daughter,
I see those paintings now, many
canvases done in your quick strokes,
your sudden realizations, where I
walk sleepless in a dark gallery
on hot nights in Pittsburgh.

Faxes to William

For Stephen Dobyns

ONE

Some poets write blurbs, William,
and some do not. And it is by
a law of nature that the former
envy the latter desperately
though they, the former, can do
nothing to release themselves
from the trap, squirm and prevaricate
as they may. They have unmade
their beds and they must schlep in them.

TWO

The news announces that research now shows
aspirin to be a preventative for certain cancers.
Joe-Anne who every morning insists she has a
headache cries out in glee,
"You see!
I've been doing the right thing for years!"

THREE

The man who has a lifelong intimate relationship
with death, who thinks of death continually,
whose sexual and esthetic behavior is determined
by death, whose ordinary perceptions and routines
of work are shadowed by death, nevertheless
hides his obsession or disguises it in hundreds
of devious and nearly unconscious demeanors,
and then he wonders, he always wonders,
if everyone else is doing the same thing.

FOUR

William, you are a fisherman. It seems
as if all my friends are fishermen.
You know every trout stream and salmon river
in New England, the Maritimes, and Michigan.
You sit in your tiny room with hundreds of
boxes of feathers, wires, fabric, I don't know what,
and tie flies, exquisite flies, works of art,
which you frame behind glass for your friends,
and at night when you dream as like as not
it's of some particular stretch of shining water
you've read about in Scotland or Peru.
William, I hate fishing. I hate to kill.
Killing even a nearly brainless pike or a
totally brainless broccoli unnerves me. I long
to come to nature not as an intruder killing
and ravaging but as a compleat insider, one
of the fraternity, paid up and at my ease
forever. But I hate to kill. William, how
can we be friends? How can I be a poet?

FIVE

In this transition, William,
        from winter to spring
today in the pasture
        I was up looking

at the run-off, the damage
        of wash-out and rivulet.
That pasture is about
        as wet as it can get.

It's almost as if the sea
        withdrew from the strand

this morning, leaving me
        this new found land.

Well, you know that
        long low spot
crossways on the downside
        of the ledge outcrop?

It was still full of snow.
        Snow lay in the swale
of my hill pasture
        like Ahab's white whale.

SIX

I came to this nearly anonymous
town, William, four years ago
to make myself completely anonymous,
me with my social security and my
little house on the hill. And now?
These nearly anonymous bastards
have increased my assessment 3.5
times. That's three point five! Taking
advantage of an exiled poet, the shits.
They better watch out, I'll spread their
rotten town all over the map for the rest
of time! Well, for a few years anyway.

SEVEN

William, when the cat
starts to throw up
– convulsing and gagging –
there's really nothing to do
but sit still and watch it.

EIGHT

When a bug flies into your mouth,
William, and dies and you
can't get it out so eventually
you swallow it, afterward
for an hour you still feel
a little nasty after-lump
in the middle of your throat.

NINE

William, where the dancing saffron
butterfly disappeared within
the shadow of the sumac
grove I saw
the apparition of a hideous naked
old man peering out.

TEN

Every year, William,
I say I'll note
not the first but the last
firefly of the season,
but then they're gone,
vanished undetected.
Tonight is motionless.
Where they go, William,
is what we know, not when.
Does it make any difference?

ELEVEN

How the hell does a butterfly fly
against the wind? How does she

fly through the rain? Don't give me your
precise scientific answers, William.
They don't mean a thing. Precisely.

TWELVE

Weddings, William –
what are we
to think of them?
For my part at least
I'd sooner be
married by an apple tree
than by a priest.

THIRTEEN

The fallen hibiscus flower
that was so exotic, intricate, and splendid
lay on the floor, a reddish
pulpy mess. I took it
to the container of unpleasantness
for the compost heap. Inevitably,
William, I thought of
all the poems I've written.

FOURTEEN

Let me tell you, William,
something crucial, something
absolutely basic, with which
I know you'll agree. Otherwise
we have no basis for this
colloquy. Justice can never
contain injustice. I don't care
what the president says.

FIFTEEN

William, for the things
life didn't give us
we have no
compensation. None.

SIXTEEN

Nothing on land, William, nothing
Equals a storm at sea. You watch
100,000 tons of water rise
Mountainously from nowhere,
Warrump, before you, above you,
And you know what a trifling
Nervous squiggle you are in the
Cosmos of elemental energy.
Fortunately this happened to me
Fifty years ago, and since then
I've lived in monotonous delusion.

SEVENTEEN

For some of us, William,
whom you call fools and poets
the death of love is the death of life
however long the blood and breath endure.
And this is knowledge. And knowledge
cannot be dissipated
by a song.

EIGHTEEN

Sometimes, William, a swallow of coffee
goes down your esophagus like an orange
going down an ostrich. It's gross, William,

it's disconcerting. Why must we be reminded
that Nature can be as corrupt as Congress?

NINETEEN

William, do you know why
I like writing these faxes
to you? Because you
don't have a fax machine.

Good Old Word Blues

Tarry my beloved here
for a moment between
this funeral home and
this legion hall in this
american small town's
dirt and darling marry
me we can never marry
enough kiss my neck
and hold my hand for
the cop has drunk our
last beer the councilman
has said if you're dying
why don't you go to
the hospital oh tarry
a moment my dearest
here and sing the song
of your black irish blues
about wind and rock and
luck gone cold sweetheart
and how it don't take too long.

Graves

Both of us had been close
to Joel, and at Joel's death
my friend had gone to the wake
and the memorial service
and more recently he had
visited Joel's grave, there
at the back of the grassy
cemetery among the trees,
"a quiet, gentle place," he said,
"befitting Joel." And I said,
"What's the point of going
to look at graves?" I went
into one of my celebrated
tirades. "People go to look
at the grave of Keats or Hart
Crane, they go traveling just to
do it, what a waste of time.
What do they find there? Hell,
I wouldn't go look at the grave
of Shakespeare if it was just
down the street. I wouldn't
look at – " And I stopped. I
was about to say the grave of God
until I realized I'm looking at it
all the time....

Waterloo

Overlooking the battlefield, on that grassy
ridge where the ladies and gentlemen of Brussels
brought their servants and picnic hampers
and card tables to watch, you could smell
the exploding gunpowder and hear shrieks
in the distance, you could see the brightly
uniformed bodies of men running and firing,
clashing their swords and falling,
and he became ill. He couldn't help it. His hands
trembled, his mouth trembled, he retched
and vomited over a picnic table, he tried to drink
from a bottle of champagne and spilled it
down the front of his shirt, he soiled his trousers.
It was unbelievable, atrocious. He felt worse
than he could say. He went from table to table,
seeking comfort or reassurance, he didn't know what.
The ladies in colorful dresses and huge hats,
the gentlemen in brilliantly tailored suits
were talking and smiling, looking through their
opera glasses, pointing here and there to explain
tactics and mark the approach of fresh legions
on either side. But they paid no attention
to him, they couldn't hear him or see him,
as if he were invisible, *un citoyen*
d'autrefois. The smell thickened,
the stench choked him, and the screams
of the dying men and horses became
piercing and unbearable. He looked closely
at the people around him, yet no one looked
at him. Perhaps he wasn't there. But he was.

What to Do

Tell your mind and its
　　agony
to the white bloom
　　of the blue plum tree,

a responding beauty
　　irreducible
of the one earth and ground,
　　for real.

Once a year
　　in April
in this region
　　you may tell
　　for a little while.

Notes on Poverty

Was I so poor
    in those damned days
that I went in the dark
    in torn shoes
and furtiveness
    to steal fat ears
of cattle corn
    from the good cows
and pound them
    like hard maize
on my worn Aztec
    stone? I was.

Song: Now That She is Here

for Joe-Anne

An old man now, who's learned at last
What it means truly to be in love.
    Ah, all those years of the past –
    I used to think I knew but I didn't know.

Like a neophyte in the school of lust,
    Struggling with shame and doubt,
        I fell and lay low,
Because I thought I knew when I didn't know.

    Old age is failure. Natural
Exhaustion, mind and body letting go,
Words misremembered, ideas frayed like old silk.
       But I am in love now,
    In it totally all the time.
I have nothing else, I have forgotten my name,
    I live on taters, whiskey, and goat's milk
      In a little house by the wood
While a cold wind rises and the night fills with snow,
    Who used to think I knew. But now I know.

The Beat

Well, I'm too much of a musician
To throw away the beat. After all
It's running in my head, that
Tsep-tsep-tsep of the tenor drum,
The bass riding easy beside it.
Obviously it's not the only
Way to walk, but it's how I
Walk, trucking along the lane
Of lilacs in the springtime.

In the Long Hall

On his knees he was weaving a tapestry
which was unraveling behind him. At first
he didn't mind it; the work was flawed,
loose ends, broken threads, a pattern
he could not control; but as his skill
improved he began to resent the way
his tapestry was undoing itself.
He resolved not to look back
but to keep going ahead, as he did
successfully for a long time. Still
later, however, he began to notice
that the part of the tapestry in front
of him was unraveling too; threads
he had just knotted became loose.
He tied them again. But before long
he could not keep up, his hands
were too slow, his fingers too weak.
The unraveling in front pushed
him toward the unraveling in back
until he found himself isolated
on a small part of the tapestry whose
pattern he could not see because
it was beneath his own body. He spun
this way and that. He worked as fast as
he could with trembling fingers
in futility, in frenzy, in despair.

The Woods

Finally the woods
are stripped down
and the great trees
are gone,

leaving a tangle
of saplings and vines,
used up and ugly,
confused signs

of the simplicities
that once were here,
the high crowns for tanagers,
glades for the deer.

This Morning

after Wang Wei

Winter ending in the field, snowcrust thrust
into gray grass. Two crows flopped
to the bare ash, black, and raised their heads
and shouted, and the hillside resounded. Just
last night Wang Wei said, "No looking back."

Thorntrees

A corner of my woods is thorn,
Sprung up where grander trees were cut,
So thick, cohesively earthborn
I cannot penetrate it, but

I know who's alive in there.
I hear them sing and work and die,
The multitude in a tangly lair
Protected from my awful eye.

Apart, alone on a summer eve,
I smoke my cigarette and cough,
Acknowledging what I believe
Till gnats and black flies drive me off.

In Georgetown

Holiday Inn, Washington, D.C.

This is not where the rich and famous pursue their lifestyles.

This is exactly like the Holiday Inn in Troy, N.Y., where I stayed
    recently.

It is near enough to exactly like the Holiday Inn where I stayed in
    Tucson,

In Casper, in Chillicothe, in Opelika, in Portsmouth, in Bellingham,
    etc.

A mirror in a fake gilt frame, brass bed lamps attached to the wall by
    hinges.

"Fax Your Urgent Documents To or From This Holiday Inn Hotel."

All at once the smoke alarm goes off for no reason. *Eeeeeeeeeeee!*

Thumps on the door, an anxious black lady. "Are you all right in there,
    sir?"

I climb on a brocaded chair and disconnect the smoke alarm ruthlessly.

Meanwhile rich and famous men are pursuing their lifestyles two
    blocks away

In four-story Federal brick houses with porticoes and flagstone steps.

Fucking each other's wives in dens and laundry rooms and pantries.

This is called a party. Some are Democrats, some Republicans, all are
    fuckers.

They are emboldened by bourbon and vodka and the anticipation of
    power.

Tomorrow they will arise hungover and wield the resources of the
    nation.

Sweetheart, so far from home I'm thinking of you as much as I can.

Melodiously at the door: "Are you all right, sir? Are you all right
    in there?"

Prepare

"Why don't you write me a poem that will prepare me for your
    death?" you said.

It was a rare day here in our climate, bright and sunny. I didn't feel like
    dying that day,

I didn't even want to think about it – my lovely knees and bold
    shoulders broken open,

Crawling with maggots. Good Christ! I stood at the window and I saw
    a strange dog

Running in the field with its nose down, sniffing the snow, zigging and
    zagging,

And whose dog is that? I asked myself. As if I didn't know. The limbs
    of the apple trees

Were lined with snow, making a bright calligraphy against the world,
    messages to me

From an enigmatic source in an obscure language. Tell me, how shall I
    decipher them?

And a jay slanted down to the feeder and looked at me behind my glass
    and squawked.

Prepare, prepare. Fuck you, I said, come back tomorrow. And here he
    is in this new gray and gloomy morning.

We're back to our normal weather. Death in the air, the idea of death
    settling around us like mist,

And I am thinking again in despair, in desperation, how will it happen?
    Will you wake up

Some morning and find me lying stiff and cold beside you in our bed?
    How atrocious!

Or will I fall asleep in the car, as I nearly did a couple of weeks ago,
    and drive off the road

Into a tree? The possibilities are endless and not at all fascinating,
    except that I can't stop

Thinking about them, can't stop envisioning that moment of hideous
    violence.

Hideous and indescribable as well, because it won't happen until it's
    over. But not for you.

For you it will go on and on, thirty years or more, since that's the
distance between us
In our ages. The loss will be a great chasm with no bridge across it
(for we both know
Our life together, so unexpected, is entirely loving and rare). Living
on your own –
Where will you go? what will you do? And the continuing sense of
displacement
From what we've had in this little house, our refuge on our green or
snowbound
Hill. *Life is not easy and you will be alive.* Experience reduces itself to
platitudes always,
Including the one which says that I'll be with you forever in your
memories and dreams.
I will. And also in hundreds of keepsakes, such as this scrap of a poem
you are reading now.

Little Citizen, Little Survivor

A brown rat has taken up residence with me.
A little brown rat with pinkish ears and lovely
almond-shaped eyes. He and his wife live
in the woodpile by my back door, and they are
so equal I cannot tell which is which when they
poke their noses out of the crevices among
the sticks of firewood and then venture farther
in search of sunflower seeds spilled from the feeder.
I can't tell you, my friend, how glad I am to see them.
I haven't seen a fox for years, or a mink, or
a fisher cat, or an eagle, or a porcupine, I haven't
seen any of my old company of the woods
and the fields, we who used to live in such
close affection and admiration. Well, I remember
when the coons would tap on my window, when
the ravens would speak to me from the edge of their
little precipice. Where are they now? Everyone knows.
Gone. Scattered in this terrible dispersal. But at least
the brown rat that most people so revile and fear
and castigate has brought his wife to live with me
again. Welcome, little citizen, little survivor.
Lend me your presence, and I will lend you mine.

Scrambled Eggs and Whiskey

Scrambled eggs and whiskey
in the false-dawn light. Chicago,
a sweet town, bleak, God knows,
but sweet. Sometimes. And
weren't we fine tonight?
When Hank set up that limping
treble roll behind me
my horn just growled and I
thought my heart would burst.
And Brad M. pressing with the
soft stick, and Joe-Anne
singing low. Here we are now
in the White Tower, leaning
on one another, too tired
to go home. But don't say a word,
don't tell a soul, they wouldn't
understand, they couldn't, never
in a million years, how fine,
how magnificent we were
in that old club tonight.

HAYDEN CARRUTH was born in 1921 and for many years lived in northern Vermont. He lives now in upstate New York, where until recently he taught in the Graduate Creative Writing Program at Syracuse University. He has published twenty-nine books, chiefly of poetry but including also a novel, four books of criticism, and two anthologies. His most recent books are *Selected Essays & Reviews, Collected Longer Poems, Collected Shorter Poems, 1946–1991*, and *Suicides and Jazzers*. He has been editor of *Poetry*, poetry editor of *Harper's*, and for 20 years an advisory editor of *The Hudson Review*. He has received fellowships from the Bollingen Foundation, the Guggenheim Foundation, and the National Endowment for the Arts, and a 1995 Lannan Literary Fellowship. He has been presented with the Lenore Marshall Award, the Paterson Poetry Prize, the Vermont Governor's Medal, the Carl Sandburg Award, the Whiting Award, and the Ruth Lily Prize, among many others, and he has been nominated for the Pulitzer Prize and the National Book Award. In 1992 he was awarded the National Book Critics' Circle Award for *Collected Shorter Poems, 1946–1991*.

BOOK DESIGN and composition by John D. Berry, using Adobe PageMaker 6.0 and a Power Computing Power 120. The type is Janson Text, a digital adaptation by Adrian Frutiger of the 17-century type of Hungarian punch-cutter Nicholas Kis. Kis spent ten years working in Amsterdam, and his type is one of the sturdy old-style typefaces typical of Dutch printing of the period. In the 20th century, it was adapted for hot-metal composition and widely used in fine books. The revived typeface was called "Janson" because it was mistakenly attributed at first to Anton Janson, a Dutch typographer who worked in Leipzig. Janson Text retains many of the idiosyncrasies of the original design and maintains its legibility at text sizes. *Printed by Edwards Brothers.*